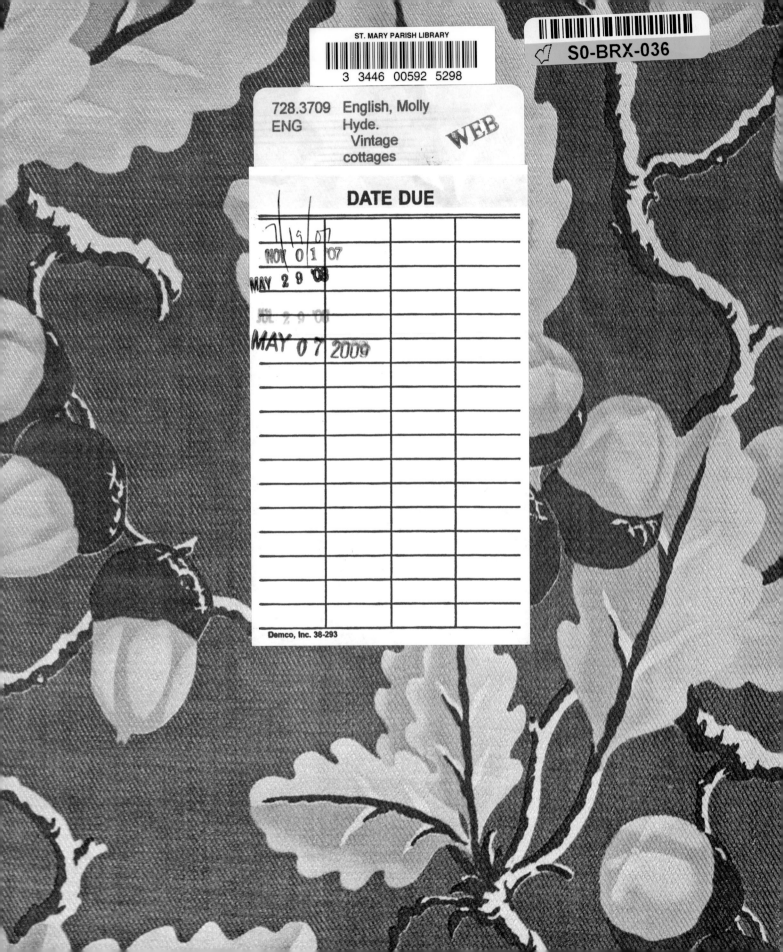

A. R. DILLS
1888

vintage cottages

MOLLY HYDE ENGLISH

Photography by TOM LAMB

Gibbs Smith, Publisher

TO ENRICH AND INSPIRE HUMANKIND

Salt Lake City | Charleston | Santa Fe | Santa Barbara

First Edition
11 10 09 08 07   5 4 3 2 1

Text © 2007 Molly Hyde English
Photographs © 2007 Tom Lamb

Published by
Gibbs Smith, Publisher
P.O. Box 667
Layton, Utah 84041

Orders: 1.800.835.4993
www.gibbs-smith.com

Designed by Glyph Publishing Arts
Printed and bound in China

Library of Congress Cataloging-in-Publication Data
English, Molly Hyde.
  Vintage cottages / Molly Hyde English ; photographs by Tom Lamb. — 1st ed.
    p. cm.
  ISBN-13: 978-1-4236-0142-5
  ISBN-10: 1-4236-0142-4
  1. Cottages—United States. 2. Second homes—United States. 3. Vacation homes—United States.
I. Lamb, Tom. II. Title.
NA7561.E54 2007
728'.370973—dc22

2006038209

NOT LONG AFTER THE PUBLICATION of *Camps and Cottages*, I received a call from my husband, Rich. "I'm at the plaza standing with animal control Officer Rogers, and she's just introduced me to the most soulful pup I've ever met!" I knew in an instant that our family was about to grow. Yet I paused and asked him if he was certain and how he thought an additional dog might sit with the other two. "Beautifully—I know it! Listen, Molly, he's been sitting with other rescue pets in a daze, but when our eyes met, he lit up. I gave him a nose-kiss, asked Officer Rogers if I might walk him and over the course of that walk we bonded!" I asked Rich what he knew about his new-found friend and his response sealed the deal, "He was found abandoned on a busy road. He was in tough shape when they found him, but a local vet has patched him up. He's an older guy, and many of the younger families have passed him by. I can't bear to see him return to the pound. You've got to trust me on this one." Trust him, I did, and neither of us, including Labradors Hannah and Charlie, ever looked back. We named him "Buddy," and within days he had claimed a favorite club chair as his own and slept close by at night. For eighteen wonderful months, Buddy held center stage. He and Rich took weekend day trips together as well as walks along the beach. He was even featured on a television episode of HGTV! Looking back, I think Rich and I, despite our endless joy with Buddy, sensed that time with him might be too short. And so it was when just before our second Thanksgiving together we lost him to an incurable tumor. On our last day with him we cried uncontrollably and were sure that our sorrow would never end. But we turned to Hannah and Charlie and held them close. Their unqualified love helped us heal. We've learned firsthand that the warmth of a home and the presence of a loved pet go hand in hand. To you Buddy—my angel boy—I dedicate this book.

Acknowledgments

THOUGH ONE MAY HAVE BEEN fortunate to have a book published in the past, there is never an expectation that another will follow. It takes an interesting angle and fresh story line but most importantly the interest and guidance of an editor with the courage to say "yes" and the chutzpah to say "no." Suzanne Taylor was with me the first time and, along with Hollie Keith, has stuck with me the second. Thank you, Suzanne and Hollie. You're consummate professionals and steadfast taskmasters.

Attracting a photographer who shares your vision is always challenging. I'm grateful to have worked with Tom Lamb. East Coast bred but now living on the West Coast, Tom has established himself as an accomplished artist, photographer and teacher. He shares with his wife, Vickie, a classic early-twentieth-century seaside cottage and a passion for life fashioned around all things natural and sustainable. Because of that passion, he has been able to make the connection between the intimacy of cottages, the natural touches of those who choose to live in them, the colorful gardens that surround them and the family pets that roam within them. To Tom and his staff, Terry Miller and Michelle Leighton, a heartfelt thanks for your discerning eyes and unquestionable talent.

The life of a shopkeeper, stylist and author often borders on the routine. That's not to say that I don't enjoy growing and nurturing the business I launched in Berkeley years ago, but it's the unexpected note of encouragement that keeps me charging ahead. Shortly after moving Camps and Cottages to Laguna Beach, I received visits, mostly during the summer months, from a woman for whom I have tremendous respect. I knew her to be a busy mom and a person at the top of her profession. I was always attentive but never intrusive, and was grateful for her business. Over time we began to chat, she introduced herself and has subsequently been a great source of encouragement. Thank you, Diane Keaton.

Thank you to all the homeowners for graciously allowing us into their homes.

A very special thanks to Marsha Alldis, who, besides being the creator of one of America's favorite destinations for French and American period pieces, Tancredi & Morgen of Carmel Valley, California, has been a key source of resources for the book.

In my opinion, no one has captured better the meaning of life, friendship and home than Simon and Garfunkel. When I hear their music, I think of those who have worked with me over the span of a decade, and I want to thank them once again for their special friendship—Lynn Cirelli, Karen Stern, Steve Reed, Susan Lamb and Katherine Garren.

Special love and thanks to my sister Mary, my life-long pal Paula Hitchcock, and Carmelita Centanni who provided encouragement and support in the early days of Camps and Cottages in Berkeley, California.

Last but not least, a special thanks to my husband, Rich, who, along with our Labrador pups Hannah and Charlie, continues to be my best friend and most ardent supporter.

Contents

Introduction: The Journey Continues **viii**

English Cottage 1

Keystone 11

Hedges West 19

Birdsong 24

Chautauqua 33

Land's End 43

Peters Gate 52

A Dog's World and Crow Corner 60

Schlegel House 66

Jane's Place 77

Magnolia Cottage 85

Shaw's Cove 94

Conroy Cottage 102

Pelican Roost 113

Painters Cottage and Fisherman's Perch 122

Resources **134**

Introduction: The Journey Continues

THE INSPIRATION FOR my first book was a child-hood family road trip in 1959 from California to Colorado. Not long after *Camps and Cottages* was published, I asked my husband, a native upstate New Yorker, what he thought of the idea of searching out old cottages and new styles by visiting some of the areas where he had grown up. I was born and raised in the greater Los Angeles area and had maintained many of the same friendships from grade school through college. My husband's childhood was radically different. He had grown up as a "company brat," and as his dad worked his way up the company ladder, it meant moving from city to city. I knew that a few of the East Coast locations might bear an interesting variety of cottage styles—from upstate New York to Philadelphia and Washington—and though the trip would be whirlwind, it would give this Californian a chance to temper "book-taught" perceptions with firsthand doses of reality.

Rich's hometown has been characterized by urban historians as a "company" town. In 1905 Henry B. Endicott and George F. Johnson purchased a failing shoe factory, revived it, and over the course of the next seventy years, provided employment to tens of thousands of locals, many of whom were European immigrants freshly processed through Ellis Island. The towns of Endicott and Johnson City, New York, sprung up around the preexisting city of Binghamton, and all three were located along the Susquehanna River. Today, hundreds of small and utilitarian homes dot the "Triple Cities," most with two bedrooms and one bath. Beginning in the late 1920s, they were constructed by the company, offered to workers at affordable prices and paid off through a payroll deduction system. Most of them remain today in relatively good shape and have changed little except for a coat of paint or new landscaping. Though neither "vintage" nor "cottage" in the traditional sense, they share with their classic cousins a sense of simplicity, utility and sustainability, and visiting them provided me with an appreciation of the enduring strength of America's workers and their belief in the sanctity of home.

As we continued our journey west to the Finger Lake region and then north and east to the Adirondacks, I discovered more of what I was looking for—the simple, unique and interestingly appointed American cottage. Harvey H. Kaiser has pointed out in his seminal work *Great Camps of the Adirondacks*, that the region is filled with great lodges and camps—from Kill Kare to Carolina and Pine Knot. I elected, however, to focus on the shapes, styles and colors of the small places and was pleased to see that colors like camp red and forest green prevailed among many of them. The exteriors varied from plain to storybook to stone. A peek inside a few of them revealed interiors constructed of everything from lathe and plaster to knotty pine to stone, but it also revealed some surprises. Where I would have envisioned living rooms to be bathed in rustic tradition, more than a few displayed refined tastes, sparse spaces and modern interiors including flat-panel screens and home office equipment. It's obvious that even the humblest of America's cottages have gone digital in a very big way!

We headed south into Pennsylvania and through another early industrial mainstay—the anthracite coal region, where again the plain and uni-colored structures reflected the toil and determination of another American worker—the miner. At the end of a long day on the road, we arrived in Bucks County, Pennsylvania, a colonial community abounding in the arts, i.e. Pearl Buck and the New Hope Art Festival and in history, i.e. Washington's crossing of the Delaware during the Revolutionary War. The area sits just north of Philadelphia. We found scores of cottages tucked between early colonials. Rich excitedly found the street where he had lived during junior high school and pointed out a small stone cottage in the distance. Originally used as an auxiliary structure, it sat near a larger home built, according to locals, in 1690. Surrounded by woods and a field complete with horses, the stone cottage still harbors original wrought-iron bars on several of the windows in what is now a kitchen. Intended as a line of last defense in skirmishes between early European settlers and Native Americans, seeing those bars provided me with an authentic glimpse of early American history while the juxtaposition of iron bars with the rest of the cottage made for an interesting contrast between old and new.

Our whirlwind journey ended in Washington, D.C., where Rich had attended school, and while known more for its colonial architecture than for cottage simplicity, the area was also full of surprises. While walking near our hotel at Dupont Circle, we discovered that a local group was conducting a home tour to raise money for the restoration of a historical structure. Though most of the dozen or so homes offered up a Federalist sensibility, the interior of one eighteenth-century townhome contained three floors of vibrant color, art and furniture. In fact, each of the twelve rooms sported a different hue, and though it sounds radical, it worked! It reinforced my belief in the power of color and in the conviction that art and furniture, however sparse, is at its best when placed against a colored background as opposed to a neutral one. Though the tour focused on townhomes and not cottages, I left Washington, heading home with a sense of excitement. Just as cottage owners across America are breaking with tradition and lending a new look to their humble spaces, so too have the owners of that Dupont Circle townhome broken with the deep-seated Federalist tradition of muted tones and royal colors, and something tells me that their breakthrough is just the beginning!

English Cottage

THE SON OF A GERMAN immigrant, Gustav Laumeister had, by 1900, earned the reputation as one of Palo Alto, California's master builders. Nearby Stanford University, only a few years old at the time, was in the midst of a campaign to attract the very best faculty, primarily from the Ivy League. The school's administration determined that in addition to competitive salaries, superb facilities, academic freedom and a warm year-round climate, the tipping point for scholars used to East Coast comfort would be homes that reflected tradition and modest luxury. Laumeister and several contemporaries answered the call with the creation of a neighborhood just east of campus. Unlike nearby homes constructed mostly of stucco and with Mediterranean lines, Laumeister's homes were wooden clapboard or shingle with a strong East Coast feel. Over a hundred years later, that historically protected neighborhood, home to academics and technology magnates alike, is intact and endearingly referred to as "Professorville." With his Palo Alto task completed the then sixty-year-old Laumeister looked south to the central California Coast and Carmel-by-the-Sea. The year was 1925. He selected a lot five blocks from the historic Carmel Mission and nine blocks from Carmel Bay, and employed the same East Coast touches that he had used in Professorville, but on a much smaller scale.

The dining room table holds a vintage concrete California bear. A series of turn-of-the-century plein air paintings of California poppies balances the room.

Redwood framed and wood shingled, the 1,500-square-foot cottage sits above street level on a terraced 7,800-square-foot lot. The structure is tucked amidst majestic oak, pine and holly trees. Laumeister's choice of proportion between cottage and lot ensured an almost parklike feel to the property. The original walkways that he laid throughout the property, all of which are made of Carmel stone, remain shipshape after eighty years. The current owners, in collaboration with a locally established and respected family of contractors, have restored the cottage exactly in the manner in which Laumeister would have remembered it in 1925.

Entry to the property is made through a grape-stake gated fence adorned with mature ivy. The stone paths weave around and up a

OPPOSITE: A subtle floral wreath hangs from the aged grape-stake gate to the property. ABOVE: The century-old stone path winds through more than fifty species of flowers, plants and trees on the way to the cottage's intimate front courtyard.

The paths run through a **wild English garden** with dozens of varieties of plants and flowers, planted in a way that **colorful blooms will be staged** throughout the year.

The living room is warmed by a wood-burning fireplace and early-twentieth-century leather chairs around a table hand-crafted by artisan Steve Reed. A handful of early-twentieth-century American oil paintings accent the walls.

slight terraced grade to the cottage. The paths run through a wild English garden designed by Bay Area artisans Steve Reed and Tim Lipinski. The garden contains dozens of varieties of plants and flowers, planted in a way that colorful blooms will be staged throughout the year, with special emphasis on roses. Though not yet mature, the climbing roses will one day encircle the

original wood windows and french doors pointing into the front brick courtyard.

Designed intentionally to separate living space from entertainment space, the cottage is horseshoe shaped with an extended hallway connecting the two "wings." Entry is made through a beveled-glass dutch door. The warm cream-colored interior is constructed of original board and batten

throughout and contrasts with the light amber hues of the fir floor. To the right is a comfortable living room. The north end of the living room is floor-to-ceiling bookshelves within which the owner has tucked vintage pottery, books, collectibles and early-twentieth-century oil paintings. The east wall contains the fireplace constructed of Carmel stone and a simple white wood mantel. To one side of the mantel, circa 1920s and 1930s oil paintings are hung, one of which is a portrait by noted California artist Philip Newberg. Above the mantel is a camp scene in oil on board painted most likely by a magazine illustrator in the 1930s (the name is unknown). On the opposite side, an original Navajo blanket hangs with reds and dark browns in contrast to the

LEFT: Vintage still life featuring a 1930s basket, handcrafted birch bark canoe and 1920s collegiate trophies. A vintage camp lamp highlights the circa-1930 portrait by noted California artist Philip Newberg. TOP: Contrasting colors and cultures abound between the early-twentieth-century Navajo rug and a Maryland football pillow from the same period. ABOVE: A rare 1914 New York baseball trophy pairs up with a silver bowl filled with vintage carnival balls.

LEFT: The intimate guest cottage located adjacent to the main house is brightened by a classic Pendleton blanket. The entry to the kitchenette is defined by a floor-to-ceiling baseball banner from Pennsylvania. ABOVE: The master bedroom is defined with bold camp and Navajo blankets and amber-toned camp lamps. The oil painting under the lamp is a late 1920s self-portrait by California artist Axel Linus and sits below a primitive American Indian painting dated 1933.

cream-colored walls. The southernmost wall is floor-to-ceiling french bay windows that push out to enhance the flow of ocean breezes throughout the house. The west wall contains original french doors for entry into the front courtyard.

The separate dining room is filled with a mid-nineteenth-century cabinet as well as a Steve Reed–designed table surrounded by Old Hickory chairs. Atop the table is a vintage concrete California bear. The kitchen (not pictured), just off the dining room, has been completely restored with new appliances, hardwood floors and indirect lighting.

Just off the hallway on the way to the master bedroom, at the other end of the horseshoe, are a pair of "Jack and Jill" guest bedrooms. Hanging colorfully in the corner of one bedroom is a 1940s oil painting by Marybelle Schmidt Bigelow. The bedrooms

Tucked away just off of the main cottage is a tiny but comfortable guest cottage. The owners use it as a getaway to read and write. A sporty 1940 baseball banner separates the living area from kitchenette and half bath.

TOP: Charlie and his buddy Hannah keep a close watch over birds, squirrels and other guests on the parklike property. ABOVE: A 1940s oil painting by Marybelle Schmidt Bigelow brightens a bedroom corner. RIGHT: A guest bedroom features a bed and side table from Maine Cottage Furniture lighted by newly crafted wood camp sconces. The circa-1920 primitive oil paintings contrast beautifully against the earth-toned bed cover. OPPOSITE: Each bathroom in the 1925 home has been updated with new fixtures and plumbing while maintaining the cottage's original feel.

are anchored by a newly restored bathroom with period octagonal tile on the floor and subway tile around the tub and shower. The only new addition, a skylight, allows tree-filtered sunlight and shadows to brighten the small space. The darkly framed vintage mirror contrasts beautifully with the cream walls.

Around the corner, the master bedroom is flooded with sunlight through wood push-out windows and a bank of original french doors facing east into the front courtyard. The portrait on the nightstand is a 1920s self-

portrait by California artist Axel Linus. The master bathroom has, like its guest counter-part, been fully restored with the same look.

Tucked away just off of the main cottage is a tiny but comfortable guest cottage. The owners use it as a getaway to read and write. A sporty 1940 baseball banner separates the living area from kitchenette and half bath.

Colorful, bright and airy, and a perfect place for the owners' Labradors, Hannah and Charlie, this cottage was born of simplicity and remains so to this day! ◆

Keystone

THIS 1935 RETREAT serves as a getaway for Wendy and Larry Steinberg. Larry, who is on the faculty at Temple University in Philadelphia, has worked with Wendy to restore this two-bedroom cottage in a way that might make it unrecognizable to its original owner. "Simplicity and comfort are the characteristics that come to mind when I think of the cottage," says Larry. Though no additions have been made to the original structure, the interior pine walls have been restored in perfect contrast to the refinished original hardwood floors, making it a perfect setting for long-held pieces and rustic appointments. "We have a mission-style oak rocker in one of the rooms that we purchased for $35 at a Wisconsin garage sale when we were first married and which, when placed in my son's nursery, was used by my husband to rock him to sleep each night," says Wendy. The bathroom has been renovated to a classic look with 1930s tiling, and the galley kitchen has been updated with professional-grade appliances, hardware and period lighting, all of which are intended to ensure the integrity of the home for decades to come. "The kitchen during the daytime is our favorite room as the sun streams against white walls and original handcrafted cabinetry," remarks Wendy.

A side view of the living room reveals the beamed ceilings and the breadth of the main room accented by a circa-1925 pond boat.

TOP: Smuckers and Lucy are Keystone's official greeters.
ABOVE: Smuckers' and Lucy's home away from home. RIGHT: A newly constructed arbor spans the front gate with a view toward a traditional red cottage door. OPPOSITE: An inviting bentwood rocker from Genesee River provides courtyard comfort.

On the far end of the living room, a group of french doors opens to a deck and view of a wooded canyon filled with wildlife and a nearby stream. Complementing the french doors is a host of latched wood windows that, when opened during the day, provide soothing breezes, helping to keep the single-wall building fresh and cool. "We

love our turn-of-the-century paintings accented at night with the hues of vintage floor lamps," Wendy notes. The pond boat in the living room is circa 1925 and once sailed the ponds of New York's Central Park. It sits adjacent a life jacket from *Minot's Light*, a yacht once owned by renowned writer Arthur Beiser, author of

Entry to the cottage is made through a gated and rose-covered trellis. The building is surrounded by a lush garden of fragrant and colorful flowers, hearty trees and abundant roses.

The Proper Yacht. The cabin sign leaning above the fireplace was purchased from an antiques dealer in Maine and lends a perfect touch to the mantel.

Entry to the cottage is made through a gated and rose-covered trellis. The building is surrounded by a lush garden of fragrant and colorful flowers, hearty trees and abundant roses. "The front brick patio is our favorite outdoor setting, particularly with our dogs, Smuckers and Lucy," comments Wendy. The herringbone brick path leads to a red front door—a true East Coast touch! ◆

ABOVE: The built-in above the fireplace contains a spectacular collection of French and American shell inkwells and boxes spanning a period from 1890 to 1930. RIGHT: A side view of the living room focuses upon the french doors leading to the deck overlooking a wooded backyard.

The master bedroom's pine walls are brightened by a vintage lime-and-grape-colored spread and lime-colored covered pillows from Utility Canvas.

The rocker adjacent the bed is from Maine Cottage Furniture and is accented with a circa-1930 trade-blanket pillow.

Hedges West

HISTORICALLY REGISTERED and designated as a "clapboard cottage," this 1921 Craftsman bungalow has undergone careful and intricate restoration. The transformation was planned and executed over a two-year period under the watchful and caring eyes of owners Kitty and Bill Fantini. Named after Hedges Lane in Amagansett, New York, where Bill grew up, the cottage sits on a rounded ledge at the top of a hillside, and has views of the sea from the new master bedroom and sitting room. Originally a barn-red structure, the Fantinis chose a muted green for the restoration, keeping with the Craftsman tradition. The front main section has been completely rebuilt and restored to its original lines, and a portion of the living room ceiling was vaulted. The rear of the home, which, when the couple purchased it, had an attached "lean-to" wing housing a small kitchen and bedroom, has been removed and replaced with a two-floor addition. The floor levels of the addition were stepped down to follow the sloping contour of the property. Bill, a graphic designer, worked so closely with his architect and builder that the end result was an addition so completely integrated that even the most discerning eye would conclude that the entire home dates to 1921.

A wide-angle view of the living room. The crispness of the walls is warmed by the hue of the cherry flooring. The still life above the fireplace is by contemporary California artist Grace Bryan.

It's hard to pick a favorite room. Each has its own best time of day with light streaming from east to west.

BELOW: A dahlia-filled Bauer vase brightens the cottage.
BOTTOM: An intimate garden and sitting area is accented by classic garden furniture, perfect for entertaining or enjoying the Sunday paper. RIGHT: Quiet dinner parties are enjoyed at Hedges West in this comfortable dining room. The oil painting above the table is a contemporary plein air. OPPOSITE: A pair of leather chairs designed by Mitchell Gold and inspired by the great French club chairs of the 1930s accent the living room.

"It's hard to pick a favorite room," says Kitty. "Each has its own best time of the day with light streaming from east to west, starting each morning in the newly built kitchen and sitting area and ending each evening in the living room." Kitty and Bill enjoy entertaining friends and family despite their busy schedule, and have built a spectacular kitchen with clean and classic lines enabling guests to watch each of them prepare traditional

recipes handed down over generations of Casales and Fantinis. In terms of interior sensibility, the couple has chosen to employ a "white and wood" design, using American cherry for the floors, dark accents of oil-rubbed bronze for hardware and a warm white for the walls. Bill notes, "Rather than using different colors for separate rooms, we have chosen to let the reflection of light 'paint' each space. The outdoor shrubbery

casts a subtle green color within the kitchen while the living room walls take on the red hue reflected off the cherry floors." The cottage has been beautifully appointed with French club chairs, an early-twentieth-century Stickley chair, Bauer pottery, a large Amish star situated just outside the rear french doors and early-twentieth-century art.

Hedges West's unique outdoor feature is its integration with the existing landscape. Just under 2,000 square feet on a 5,000-square-foot lot, a small front yard and manicured side yards lead to an intimate backyard and patio shaded by mature trees and shrubs—a perfect setting for morning espresso. ◆

The outdoor shrubbery casts a **subtle green color** within the kitchen while the living room walls take on the **red hue reflected** off the cherry floors.

Birdsong

IT'S NOT OFTEN that you hear of a person buying a classic cottage only to find out later that it was built by the grandfather of a longtime friend. That was the experience of Greg Linder when he purchased his 1929 cottage in Carmel-by-the-Sea a few years ago. Always inquisitive, Greg traced the chain of title through city records. A further scan of local reference books, particularly Linda Leigh Paul's *Cottages by the Sea*, revealed that the original builder, George Whitcomb, was considered a master builder in what was then a very small and newly emerging town. Though an addition may have been made to the structure in the 1940s, it remains pretty much as one would have found it in the late 1920s—small, simple and comfortable.

The recently trellised front door will one day welcome visitors into this intimate seaside cottage with stands of climbing roses. The original sixteen-inch redwood shingles, now painted sea-foam blue, give the home a strong New England sensibility. Greg notes, "Many visitors have asked whether it has an East Coast connection and comment how extraordinarily comfortable it is. They claim it feels as if they've stayed here in a past life." It wouldn't be surprising if guests turned on the vintage radio kept on an antique bed stand and heard Tommy Dorsey or Glenn Miller. Surreal and comfortable—now that's cottage living!

Just steps from the beach, the cottage entrance captures the feel of the sea with vintage tackle and buoys.

Good use of french doors through the cottage has turned a small home into a large and livable space—a complete outdoor-indoor solution. The brick patio, accessible from the living room and a bedroom, is surrounded by trees and coastal shrub and, when combined with the salt air of nearby Carmel Bay, makes for a potent scent that keeps guests glued to the property. Positioned around the patio are restored garden chairs from the 1930s and two original canvas beach umbrellas prevalent in the 1920s. One of the umbrellas sports an advertisement for a turn-of-the-century hardware

LEFT: One view of the guest bedroom highlights a collection of antique paddles. A primitive seascape looks down on a 1940s radio next to the colorful guest bed cover. ABOVE: An oil painting by noted Santa Fe artist Jean Jack tops the guest bed.

It wouldn't be surprising if guests turned on the vintage radio kept on an antique bed stand and heard Tommy Dorsey or Glenn Miller.

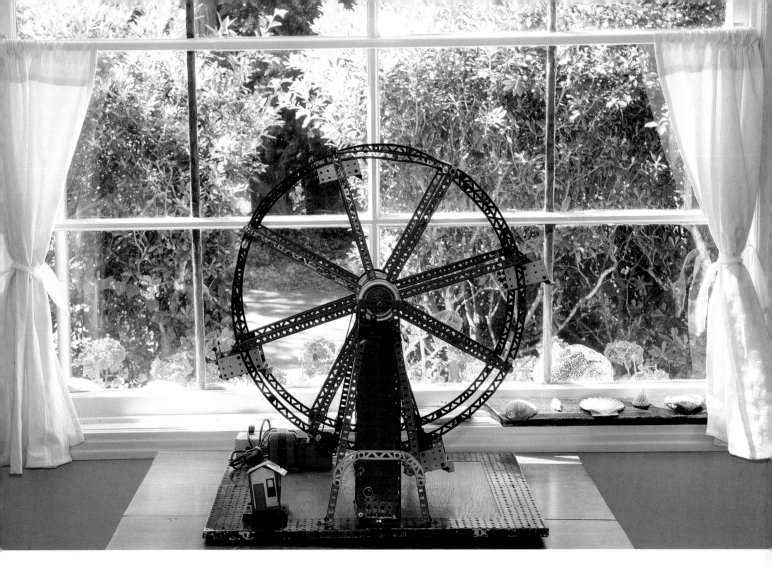

store. The oranges and greens of the chairs add a powerful dose of color and excitement to the patio. "I enjoy reading and spending long hours out here with Gus, my Jack Russell terrier. Every once and a while I pause and imagine the likes of John Steinbeck and Jack London walking by the house," says Greg. Not a far-fetched idea as both writers frequented the young town during its earlier Bohemian days.

Parked nearby is a small classic Airstream trailer that Greg uses on vacation trips from time to time. It was completely stocked and ready to go the day Tom Lamb and I visited. Greg was busy during our visit loading armfuls of classic 1930 game boards. Greg noted, "The wonderful thing about Airstream ownership is the camaraderie amongst owners. We'll drive all day and land a spot in a park around late afternoon. After breaking out the lawn chairs, table, board games, beverages and snacks, and lighting a campfire, it won't be long before fellow "Airstreamers" gather for an evening of great conversation around the campfire." Happy trails, Greg and Gus!

OPPOSITE: Vintage tackle adorns several outside walls and the surrounding fence. ABOVE: A 1940s multicolored Erector Ferris wheel works perfectly as a folk art piece within the cottage.

The salt air of nearby Carmel Bay makes for a potent scent that keeps guests glued to the property.

ABOVE: Inside a classic Airstream trailer, 1930s board games are readied for an upcoming trip. RIGHT: A colorful and perfect patio setting accented by a hard-to-find 1920 canvas umbrella.

Chautauqua

IN 1874, ALONG THE BANKS of an upstate New York lake, John Vincent and Lewis Miller, one a Methodist minister and the other a prominent businessman, established a summer institute dedicated to meditation, spiritual development, education and the arts. They named the institute Chautauqua. Soon thereafter, assemblies of like-minded persons gathered in communities throughout the country, primarily during the summer, and were taught and entertained by traveling Chautauquas. At the same time Chautauqua was established in New York, a Methodist summer camp was being established where the town of Pacific Grove, California, now stands on Monterey Bay. So successful was this summer destination that in the summer of 1879 the Chautauqua Literary and Scientific Circle was established. Its permanency gave rise to the construction of intimate summer cottages. Fast forward about a hundred years. Carmel Valley designer and store owner Marsha Alldis, her husband, Roger, their two young daughters, Megan and Gwyneth, their springer spaniels and a menagerie of cats were hunting for the perfect cottage when they came across this historic home. It was a tight fit but the couple fell in love with it at first sight, and Marsha knew that it would be the perfect setting for her classic touch—something she calls "tattered simplicity."

A grand antique mirror makes a statement above the fireplace mantel in the living room. The pond boat is an early twentieth century model and is flanked by faux bois candleholders.

33

It was **a tight fit** but the couple fell in love with it **at first sight**, and Marsha knew that it would be the perfect setting for her classic touch—something she calls **"tattered simplicity."**

Entering the property past a classic picket fence, one immediately notices the sweet scents of perennials, succulents and tropicals. The clapboard exterior is painted in a muted coral to reflect the natural setting and, to counter the fact that a good part of the year is dressed in grey due to ocean fog, the couple has employed color throughout the interior rooms. The living room is bathed in a bold primrose yellow and the bathroom in a strong coral.

The day we visited, Henry was resting in the living room on a classic antique French couch facing a colorful early-twentieth-century folk art Ferris wheel. "The main living area is on the upper floor, and we enjoy leaving the dutch door open to take full advantage of the sea breezes off the bay," Roger noted. Marsha knew that storage would be a challenge throughout the cottage, and she has tackled it well with built-in shelving and antique English and French

BELOW: Reminiscent of the French countryside, this antique farm table has likely been a focal point for over 100 years of family gatherings, continuing with Marsha, Roger and their daughters. OPPOSITE: A colorful boots and baskets collection.

A true Francophile, Marsha adds family photos to her European collectibles.

armoires and cabinets. The shelves are abundantly stocked with Marsha's favorite pottery. "I was drawn to Quimper faience pottery at age fifteen and have been collecting it ever since. It's fired in a small town situated in Brittany province at the northwestern-most tip of France. I love the primitive and pasty quality of the clay and the simplicity of its designs that began in the late seventeenth century with the creations of Jean-Baptiste Bousquet." Marsha shows the same passion in her favorite room, the studio, developing vintage clothing and fabrics for home interiors.

Lodged on the mantel with a mid-nineteenth-century mirror is an early-twentieth-century pond boat, both of which are balanced by faux bois candlesticks. Throughout the house is a spectacular collection of vintage dog paintings, serving as a

constant reminder of the synergies that have always existed between vintage cottages and great dogs.

Says Marsha, "Roger takes several 'antique hunting' trips to Europe each year, and though most of the items are earmarked for my store, I pull out many of the unique items and take them to our cottage for early enjoyment. Roger, the consummate businessman, would like everything to head to the store, but I generally win the battle." Marsha's creative genius has helped the couple maintain the Chautauqua tradition by merging the sensibilities of eighteenth- and nineteenth-century Europe with the simplicity of early-twentieth-century American architecture and design. ◆

ABOVE, LEFT: Marsha's porcelain dogs surround a photo of Maddie and an electric canine doll. ABOVE, RIGHT: Marsha designed this dress years ago for a daughter's Halloween party.

Throughout the house is a spectacular collection of **vintage dog paintings,** serving as a constant reminder of the **synergies** that have always existed between vintage **cottages** and **great dogs.**

LEFT: Marsha's home is colorful inside and out. An angle from the corner of the living room captures her collections, including a vintage deer atop a half table. ABOVE: Henry rules the household.

The **clapboard exterior** is painted in a **muted coral** to reflect **the natural setting** and, to counter the fact that a good part of the year is dressed in grey **due to ocean fog**, the couple has employed **color throughout** the interior rooms.

OPPOSITE: A strong salmon tone contrasts beautifully against the white porcelain within the guest bath. ABOVE: A true Chautauqua cottage has been brought back to life by Marsha and Roger.

Land's End

IN THE LATE nineteenth century, scores of American artists from small towns and large cities alike ventured to Europe, particularly to Paris, to study at the feet of Europe's great teachers at academies such as Julian, Colarossi and the School of Beaux Arts. When they returned, they chose to relocate in a number of emerging artists colonies; some located in the East in and around New York and Boston, and others located in the newly emerging West. Many chose the West because of the intensity of its light, the diversity of its topography and a belief that open spaces meant more freedom to be creative and room to be different. Colonies sprung up in and around Puget Sound, Portland, the Bay Area, the Monterey Bay, Santa Barbara, Los Angeles, Laguna Beach and La Jolla.

Land's End, located in Laguna Beach, California, was constructed in 1930 and is a great example of an artist's cottage of that period. Located in a heavily wooded canyon with streams running nearby, its three distinct rooms and single bathroom have changed little since the early days. The current owner's lineage is steeped in American history. As a result, he has remained steadfast in his desire to maintain the single-wall structure in a way that would be recognizable to its original owners.

Late-nineteenth-century ceremonial lodge chairs, pyrographically etched with deer and owls, sit on each side of the rustic stone fireplace. The teepee lamp is from the 1920s and came from a roadside inn in upstate New York. The plank front door is original to the cottage.

Viewed from the street, the cottage sits on the crest of a gradual up-slope. Its white picket fence and abundance of roses provide a vivid border to the greenery surrounding the cottage and the brown shingles of the structure itself. The original siding has been maintained and oiled throughout the home's life and allows the whiteness of the push-out windows to make a dramatic design statement. The river-rock fireplace is original and lends great textural contrast to the shingled walls. Most unique is the roof's edge, which

LEFT: A simple deck provides a perfect wooded setting for an early weekend breakfast with friends. TOP: Front view of Land's End and its uniquely pitched roof reminiscent of the English countryside. ABOVE: The river rock chimney anchors the cottage.

has been given a "thatched" appearance with the use of shaped shingles. The curb appeal of Land's End is both simple and dramatic.

Entering the living room through a heavy plank door adorned with stained glass, guests are immediately impressed with the interior's classic arrangement. Occupying one wall is a rugged stone fireplace—a must for those chilly and foggy nights. The living room is lighted by a simple yet tasteful chandelier. A redwood alcove contrasts sharply with the cream interior. Within the alcove

sits a late-eighteenth-century still life and a collection of early-twentieth-century adventures by Zane Grey. Facing the alcove is an Old Hickory Three Hoop chair draped with a brown-and-red-striped Beacon blanket from 1940.

The bookcases contain original trade blankets from the 1930s and '40s, and the owner relaxes each evening in the Old Hickory Grove Park chair and ottoman. Antique floor lamps with mica shades custom designed by West End Light of Benecia,

OPPOSITE: The Old Hickory leather chair and ottoman sit adjacent bookshelves filled with 1930s camp blankets, decoys and various collectibles. LEFT: A vase of flowers and collectibles add to the charming setting. TOP: A vintage leaded-glass pane in the front door. ABOVE: Vintage porcupine quill baskets from eastern Canada.

RIGHT: The upgraded galley kitchen leads to a small dining nook and out to the deck, where family and guests may ponder the next "Big Catch." OPPOSITE: A Denyse Schmidt quilt outfits the bed under framed antique prints. A vintage bentwood rocker sits near the bed and some vintage banners from the owner's alma mater.

California, light the corners of the intimate living room while the small dining room table is perfectly positioned with a view of the woods. The owner is a football fan, and when friends come over, they draw straws to determine who will claim the 1930s French leather sofa—that is, unless Cool, the owner's black Labrador is already there. "When it comes to Cool and that sofa, Cool always gets first dibs," says the owner. ◆

"When it comes to Cool and that sofa,
Cool always gets first dibs."

LEFT: A birdhouse for eight makes Land's End very inviting. ABOVE: Cool,
the owner's young Labrador, attentively awaits the arrival of dinner
guests on the front porch.

Peters Gate

"MY HOME IS THE RESULT of a series of miracles." This is the way Elizabeth Murray, an award-winning author, artist, photographer, lecturer and expert on Monet's gardens in Giverney, describes her circa-1900 home. Built originally by the renowned nocturnal artist Charles Rollo Peters, her home is actually a pair of classic single-wall cottages anchored by a main house, all of which are surrounded by natural fencing and tucked within a close of fruit, pine, cypress, oak and birch trees. In 1906, Peters invited artists, left homeless by the San Francisco earthquake, to call Peters Gate home, thereby allowing them to continue with their work. He negotiated gallery space with the Del Monte Hotel, a nearby luxury resort that attracted wealthy tourists from around the world, and provided his guests with an outlet for their work while San Francisco was rebuilt. He left for France in 1909 and never returned to his sixty-acre Monterey estate.

Over the course of the next seventy-five years, the property took on several owners, none of whom afforded it the attention it deserved. Enter Elizabeth Murray. Spiritual in demeanor but with the determination, conviction and strength of a triathlete, she pursued Peters Gate in 2000. With the cottage not yet under the protection of the National Historic Trust, Elizabeth competed with

The original circa-1900 stove in perfect working condition highlights the spacious American farm kitchen and is a favorite meeting place for family and guests alike.

deep-pocket developers who spoke of significant change or destruction. With just days to act and outgunned financially by those competitors, she convinced the owners that Peters Gate deserved to remain intact, that it should receive the historic protection it deserved, that it would be

restored to its turn-of-the-century glory, that grant funding would follow and that she was the person who would make it happen. She convinced the City of Monterey to direct some historic planning funds her way. And she received funding from some local angels and convinced the sellers to carry back the

OPPOSITE: An antique chandelier is the centerpiece to the vaulted-ceiling living room. Light pours in from all directions thanks to floor-to-ceiling windows.
ABOVE: Elizabeth's work hangs throughout the house, consistent with the origins of Peters Gate.

The interior **glows with the hue** of the **amber redwood.**
Murray's studio can be found **on one level** with the end result—
her plein air paintings—displayed throughout the house.

bulk of the home loan while she put her game plan into action. She kept her word, and within a year, Peters Gate was listed in the National Historic Register. She arranged for significant structural improvement including ceiling repair, three new fireplaces and new plumbing—all with the help of Monterey architect Terry Wilson. The two adjacent structures were turned into rental units. Elizabeth has renewed Peters's original commitment to newly emerging artists and artistic sponsors by opening the structure to classes, lectures and creativity workshops—all this while working on a children's book and a follow-up book about Monet's gardens.

The multileveled landscape, lacking in character when the home was purchased, has been graced with over twenty-seven varieties of plants, trees and shrubs—most of them indigenous to the area. Nothing is wasted. When asked about a pile of old brick stacked neatly in the middle of a walkway, she responded, "That brick will be put to good use. I've spent the past six years pulling rocks and brick from one end of the property and moving them to another. I always find good use for the material." And so she has, maintaining certain Bohemian touches throughout the

LEFT: A spacious dining room runs adjacent the living room and is only steps from the great country kitchen. ABOVE: A row of antique hand-blown blue glass from the mid- to late nineteenth century provide prism-like colors based upon the sun's angle.

There are Bohemian touches throughout the property as **Peters himself might have done.** The main house, though large, has all the qualities of **a vintage cottage.**

property as Peters himself might have done—including outdoor fixtures that allow her to shower under the stars. The main house, though large, has all the qualities of a vintage cottage. The red-painted wooden structure sits unobtrusively under large shade trees with all of its rooms serving a purpose.

The interior glows with the hue of the amber redwood. Murray's studio can be found on one level with the end result—her plein air paintings—displayed throughout the house. The great room is the primary living and gathering space with friends, featuring high ceilings, floor-to-ceiling wood-paneled windows, a hearty fireplace and a magnificent chandelier. The fixture was not in existence during Peters's occupancy but would likely have been approved by the artist after listening to Elizabeth's reasons for its inclusion.

She claims that the ghost of Peters walks throughout the property—she has sensed him and so has her dog, Toulie, short for Toulouse Lautrec, an adorable ten-year-old Couton du Tular. The blending of gentle spirits across more than a century makes Peters Gate a very special place. ◆

TOP: In late afternoon, this vintage wooden chaise beckons even the busiest artist or writer and is located in a grove of century-old trees. RIGHT: The rough-hewn handcrafted mailbox was made by a local craftsman. OPPOSITE: Peters Gate, restored with loving care, continues to be a teaching and interactive venue for artists and seekers, just as it did in 1900.

A Dog's World
and
Crow Corner

EXCEPT FOR THE 1970s dance music wafting across the property and the specially constructed bright orange eighteen-inch-high dog bone–shaped "runway" constructed on this day for a special animal rescue fund-raising event—one would swear that the setting was rural France. That's how breathtakingly beautiful Susan Fox's Crow Corner is. Constructed in 1920 and just a stone's throw from jagged cliffs overlooking the Pacific, the intimate and antiques-laden cottage acts as a weekend getaway for Susan and her husband.

On the grounds are two structures—Crow Corner and a look-alike guest cottage built in 2001. Though eighty years separate the original building from the new one, a visitor would be hard pressed to tell them apart. Reminders of Susan's attention to detail and passion for authenticity abound. Walkways weave throughout the gardens, interrupted only by a stand-alone stone fire pit that the couple makes good use of throughout the year. The gardens have been planned and nurtured to work so closely with the structures that they act as mere extensions of the interior hallways and rooms, giving both cottages a complete

Nestled in a grove of cypress and pines, the original 1920 stone cottage, together with its recently constructed twin, strike a commanding yet subtle presence in the village.

60

indoor-outdoor feel. The day I visited with Tom Lamb, I found myself entering through a formal doorway, unconsciously exiting through a side french door, weaving through a connected pathway only to reenter through another door. The flow is so uninterrupted that the intimate space is transformed into a very large one very quickly. The magnificent gardens, containing dozens of perennials and coastal shrubs, are shaded by century-old cypress trees. Handcrafted benches sit

invitingly throughout the yard. A bronze crow sculpted by distinguished artist and former Chicago Art Institute teacher Eleen Auvil keeps an eye on the property.

But back to the main event—an annual fund-raiser for pet rescue. Susan loves dogs—all dogs—and is passionate in her belief that no matter their breed, age or disposition, they all deserve a good home. So, along with Curly, her trusted bulldog, she has opened Crow Corner to neighbors and dogs for

OPPOSITE: Bronze crow by Eleen Auvil. LEFT: It's a Dog's World at Crow Corner. Susan is a champion of animal rescue. The event this day is a fund-raiser for the Golden Gate Labrador Retriever Rescue organization. Dozens of dogs make themselves at home. TOP: Sam, a Crow Corner guest, sports a classic Talbot bow tie on his way to the rescue event. ABOVE: Curly oversees his domain.

The **magnificent gardens**, containing dozens of perennials and coastal shrubs, are **shaded by** century-old **cypress trees**. **A bronze crow** sculpted by distinguished artist Eleen Auvil **keeps an eye** on the property.

TOP: A magical entrance to Crow Corner. ABOVE: A spectacular foxglove is but one of dozens of flowers and trees that abound throughout the award-winning garden. RIGHT: An iron-and-glass lamp, designed just for Crow Corner, lights the way through garden paths.
OPPOSITE: The cottages are warmed by stone fireplaces. An antique etching sits above the mantel.

several years to celebrate and support animal rescue. Highlights include a doggie stroll down the bone-shaped runway, great conversations with fellow dog owners, unending treats for the dogs, classic drinks and food for the guests and a raffle with some pretty fabulous prizes. On the day of my visit, the event was dedicated to the Golden Gate Labrador Retriever Rescue. Anyone else who has spent long hours nurturing their prize garden would have fainted at the prospect of playing host to dozens of dogs—all off-leash and free to

roam as they pleased for five hours; not Susan. "I love the garden, but I love dogs even more. Besides, we've learned to re-work the beds and bushes quickly and efficiently, and within a week it's impossible to tell that the pups were even here!"

An old Russian proverb says "If you are a host to your guest, be a host to his dog also." Susan Fox has done just that with her passion for animal rescue and has established a tradition that promises to enrich the community for years to come. ◆

Schlegel House

PRIOR TO THE MEXICAN WAR, over a half-million square miles of the American southwest, occupying portions of what is today seven states, were governed and controlled by vast ranchos. The Treaty of Guadalupe Hidalgo, forged in 1848, brought the war to an end. In exchange for $15 million, the United States purchased the territory from Mexico, and over time the ranchos disappeared. This cottage was built in 1930 in an area where two vast ranchos met. In fact, a river-stone wall, built in 1890 to delineate the border between those ranchos, remains intact today and lines one side of the property.

Staying true to the property's heritage, owners Elaine and Mark Schlegel, both master gardeners who maintain a thriving landscaping business in and around Carmel Valley, California, have complemented the century-old oaks and pines with an abundant combination of roses, philadelphus and jasmine, all of which have been situated within the split redwood railings bordering the property.

"Our design sensibility centers around function and beauty—both within the cottage and upon the surrounding property," notes Elaine. Entry is made to the property through a

Clean Scandinavian and English lines and tones complement the otherwise rustic living room.

66

rustic wood-and-wrought-iron gate, above which spans a dramatic stand of pink roses. Proceeding along the up-sloped pathway, guests are immediately enveloped by a sea of violet, red and blue perennials, and sets of hand-carved wooden benches and chairs

tucked throughout. "The serenity of what we call our 'outdoor living room' is breathtaking," says Mark. "Both of us take great inspiration just sitting, watching and listening to the wildlife and the sound of strong breezes blowing through the large oaks. We've lost count

Guests are immediately enveloped by a sea of violet, red and blue perennials, and sets of hand-carved wooden benches and chairs tucked throughout.

of the many garden design ideas that have been created while sitting in this space with a cup of tea," he adds. "And, if I'm really in the mood for some special inspiration, I crawl up into a nearby tree house—no cell phones allowed!"

Placed lovingly within the yard is also a commemorative piece they call the Samurai Badminton Trophy. "The trophy commemorates sixteen years of summer celebrations," says Elaine. "During each of those summers, we have planned and organized a huge party highlighted by some very serious badminton competitions. The winners names have been engraved on the trophy, and prizes are awarded each year at the dinner banquet that follows in our garden."

The house's exterior has a true western cedar-shingled look, with an original rock fireplace and wood windows, all of which have been painted forest green to contrast beautifully with the cedar. The pine interior walls and handcrafted pine furniture and cabinetry combine to produce a feel partly

LEFT: The tranquility of the cottage is preserved by an old grape-stake fence atop a stone wall. TOP: The Samurai Badminton Trophy. ABOVE: A handcrafted mail drop just outside the property's main gate.

Scandinavian and partly English, making for a comfortable and eclectic contrast to the property's early rancho heritage. The rock fireplace maintains a commanding presence within the living room. Elaine has placed a number of treasured collectibles on the mantel as well as upon the shelves of their upgraded kitchen.

A skylight brightens the living room, and clever use of indirect lighting in the master bedroom provides a reflection of warmth and color off the vaulted pine ceiling. Proudly featured in their bedroom is a painting of Pt. Sur by California landscape artist Arturo Tello. Just as Tello has captured the quality and mood of that coastal spot, so too have Elaine and Mark, through their fine taste and graceful sensibility, captured the spirit and tranquility of the Robles Del Rio. ◆

OPPOSITE: Elaine's kitchen reflects clean northern European lines. LEFT: A vase of viburnum from the cottage's garden brightens an English pine corner desk. RIGHT: Elaine's collection of vintage pottery include pieces from Bauer and Roseville.

The **house's exterior** has a true western cedar-shingled look, with an **original rock fireplace** and wood windows, all of which have been painted **forest green** to contrast beautifully with **the cedar.**

ABOVE: The cottage's front entrance and courtyard is shadowed by a wisteria tree. RIGHT: The nearby oak has graced the property for well over a century.

Jane's Place

TUCKED BETWEEN HIP DESIGN studios, modern live-work lofts and nautical architectural firms, and barely set back from a narrow and charming thoroughfare reminiscent of Marseilles, Jane's Place is home to artist Jane Elliott. Built in 1936, when the area played host to fishermen and canneries, it is now a home, studio and gathering place for old and new friends. Jane has been a community fixture for over two decades, having earlier in life turned what was once a motorcycle repair shop into a successful garden shop. "In those years I had great fun serving locals as well as vacationing celebrities including the great Bette Midler," says Jane. When Jane decided to turn her attention to art, a third bedroom was added to allow her to take on a tenant or two, and the back garage became her studio. "I have kept in touch with several former tenants who have since married and built families of their own and who, from time to time, when in town, drop by for dinner or coffee." Such is the beauty of Jane's Place—a magnet for the gathering of people and the exchange of ideas—a radical concept in an age where Internet cuts and pastes are portrayed as original thought and where the end products of computer gaming

The cottage patio and courtyard abound with color and activity.

ABOVE: A unique folk art piece of metal on wood entitled *Dog Crossing*, by Berkeley artisan Karen Stern, hangs in the courtyard. OPPOSITE: The garden table is set for afternoon tea. Looking down upon the setting is a folk art wood carving of the American flag.

are mistaken for genius. As Jane notes, "Real genius flows only from the eye-to-eye exchanges between people. More than a few great ideas have been bantered about over a cup of coffee at my cottage."

Entry into Jane's world takes form as a glance over the front gate or peek through a pane-less window embedded in an ivy-laden front fence. The front porch and yard contain a collection of folk art, including a wooden American flag and a pair of dogs designed by Chicago Art Institute–trained and Berkeley-based artisan Karen Stern. At night, the area is lighted by a set of vintage lanterns. The living room (not pictured) is filled with books and artists' tools. Longtime

The **front porch** and yard contain a **collection of folk art**, including a wooden **American flag** and a **pair of dogs** designed by **artisan** Karen Stern.

friend Susan Lamb notes, "As inviting as Jane's living area is, nothing beats the aroma of her kitchen, particularly when she decides, early in the day, to start a large pot of spiced red beans and rice. When word goes round that Jane is cooking in the morning, it's a sure bet that the house will be filled with friends that evening. That's just the way it is at Jane's Place."

The day we visited Jane's Place, it played host to a half dozen pups while Jane and her guests visited an espresso house just down the street, to share views and talk the news. Notwithstanding all of the modern-day work that goes on around this rustic cottage, Jane's Place stands, at the end of each day, as a beacon of comfort, authenticity and friendship. ◆

OPPOSITE: A hanging settee provides comfort and enjoyment for a cup of morning java at nearby Alta Coffee, a grass roots gathering place for writers, artists, local workers and their dogs. LEFT: Betty, one of Jane's best friends, eyes a fresh crumpet during afternoon tea. RIGHT: A Saturday morning gathering of regulars in front of Jane's Place.

ABOVE: Jane is a hit with her canine pals. OPPOSITE: A nearby doorway has remained untouched for over a century.

Built in 1936, when the area played host to fishermen and canneries, it is now a home, studio and gathering place for old and new friends.

Magnolia Cottage

ON A STREET shaded by magnolia trees stands Magnolia Cottage, which dates to 1928. Owners Lynn and Rick Cirelli have given each intimate space in and outside the house its own look—with the intent of ensuring that all of them, when viewed as a whole, comprise a functional and unique cottage.

City records reveal that the cottage was not much more than 900 square feet, just enough room for a small living room, downstairs bedroom and bathroom, and upstairs bedroom. A galley kitchen was squeezed in toward the back of the house. It changed hands nine times over the nearly eighty-year period, and somewhere along the way the space was expanded to 1,500 square feet, a perfect home for Lynn, Rick and their Tibetan terrier, Samie.

Today, though looking exactly as it did in 1928 from the outside, the inside is a reflection of traditional elegance. Lynn worked with local painters to create a custom sea-foam green for the plaster portion of the walls, all of which contrast sharply with the sheen of white enamel that has been applied to the tongue-and-groove lower portions of the walls. American cherry bookcases (not pictured) line the walls of a short hallway between the living room and study-guest room. Around the corner from the

The living room is a contrast of dark and light. Atop the mantel are starfish that Lynn and Rick have collected during their walks along the nearby beach.

THIS PAGE: The front courtyard has been prepared for an intimate dinner while Samie awaits the arrival of guests. OPPOSITE: The enclosed side yard is Lynn's secret hideaway. Overlooking it are classic leaded-glass windows surrounded by Cecil Bruner roses.

study, a small room accented by original leaded-glass windows serves as a home office for Rick, a successful mortgage banker. Keeping with the clean simplicity of the cottage, the dining room is anchored with an elegant yet simple glass chandelier. The walls contain watercolors dating to the 1940s, painted by well-known artist Thelma Speed Houston.

The galley kitchen (not pictured) has been updated with the latest professional appliances, contrasting beautifully against American cherry cabinetry.

"Our favorite room is the living room with its original fireplace and intimate character," Lynn notes. "It's the only room that has remained intact and unaltered."

Enclosed by tall walls and fences covered with old-growth vines, the secret garden is actually a combination of brick courtyard, flower beds and custom wrought-iron gates.

Hardwood floors are featured throughout the cottage, and each room is flooded with sunlight through custom leaded-glass windows. "We're surrounded by gardens, old-growth hedges and century-old trees that afford us complete privacy," says Rick.

Entry to the property is made through a wrought-iron gate topped by an arbor filled with immense blooms, into what Lynn and Rick characterize as their secret garden. Enclosed by tall walls and fences covered with old-growth vines, the secret garden is actually a combination of brick

ABOVE: A living room corner overlooked by a contemporary plein air oil painting. RIGHT: The contrast of light against dark is carried into the dining room against sea-foam walls. The watercolors above the table are from the 1940s by noted artist Thelma Speed Houston.

courtyard, flower beds and custom wrought-iron gates leading from the front of the property to the sides and a rear walkway. A vintage birdbath, a wedding gift from Lynn's mother, anchors the flower beds. "We've worked hard to ensure that every square inch of our wonderful cottage is accessible and in tip-top shape," says Lynn. This even includes the construction of custom weather-sealed

outdoor closets handsomely tucked against the back wall that serve as great auxiliary storage space for the "space-challenged" structure.

"Our design sensibility focuses upon elegant simplicity," emphasizes Lynn. "We respect the heritage of our cottage and work to maximize its comfort and utility, making it open and inviting to family and friends." ◆

OPPOSITE: A large wall mirror enlarges a living room corner, and a contemporary oil painting, specially designed and framed, cleverly hides a flat-screen television. ABOVE: Gathered in the cottage study is a grouping of family memorabilia, including a vintage circa-1920 banner from Rick's alma mater.

We respect **the heritage** of
our cottage and work to
maximize **its comfort** and utility,
making it **open and inviting**
to family and friends.

LEFT: The courtyard comes alive by the candlelight and soft hues of the study.
ABOVE: Lynn highlights her collection of dog paintings and statuary with
French tulips.

Shaw's Cove

A TWO-LANE HIGHWAY connecting Laguna Beach, California, to the outside world wound around ocean-facing canyons in 1928, having been paved only a year earlier. The ravages of a world war were almost a decade behind the few hundred persons calling Laguna home. Seiners, constructed in the Lido shipyards just ten miles to the north and white wooden Dory boats from that late-nineteenth-century fleet searched for cod, sea bass, halibut and tuna just to the south and west. Artists with canvas and easel attached to backpacks scoured the cliffs and sage-scented canyons to capture local shapes, shadows, colors and tones in what was to be called California impressionism.

Scrub oak covered the hills to the east. Hundreds of square miles of pungent orange groves and working cattle ranches stretched to the north, south and east as far as the eye could see. Orange County, California, in 1928 was an idyllic setting. Citrus farmers packed their oranges in crates labeled with colorfully lithographed depictions of a coastal Shangri-la with names like Miracle, Miss Los Angeles and Sun-Tag.

This was the backdrop for Shaw's Cove, constructed in mid-1928 in a North Laguna location

The subtle and clean lines of the room's vintage furniture contrast beautifully against strong tones and colors.

ABOVE: Carefully constructed alcoves appear throughout the house, this one accented with vintage pottery. RIGHT: Early-twentieth-century D&M tile accents stairways throughout the cottage. OPPOSITE: The front entryway pours through the cottage out to the sea.

with the same name. The original owners sought refuge from an expanding and crowded Los Angeles, a full day's auto trip away in those days. Accented with bold plank beams and handcrafted doors, this home was designed to reflect Southern California's Spanish architectural heritage and the influence of the region's early ranchos. The interior was designed with soft

angles and a generous use of washed plaster to provide adequate cooling during summer months and warmth during the damp winter months.

Dozens of wood windows and glass-paned doors were employed throughout the multistoried structure to take full advantage of direct and reflected sunlight from the Pacific, just steps away.

TOP: Red is the beloved family dog and keeps close watch over all the daily activities. ABOVE: A gaggle of geese and ducks "explore" the front garden. RIGHT: A custom-designed and fired tile displayed in the house depicts the names of its original owners. OPPOSITE: Entry to the dining room is made through a spectacular set of original leaded-glass pocket doors.

It is a keen knowledge of early-twentieth-century Southern California history and architecture that drove Diane Keaton to purchase Shaw's Cove. Diane notes, "It is both special and unique and is the sole example of early-twentieth-century Spanish architecture in all of North Laguna. I had long admired the property, and when the opportunity arose to purchase it, I did so not only out of a desire to call it home but to ensure that it remained an integral part of Laguna's architectural landscape and heritage."

Entry to the cottage is made through a doorway lined with early California tile fired by the D&M Tile Company. The company was started in 1928 by Welshman John Davies and his partner, John McDonald. Though the company was relatively short-lived, the bright Moorish designs of the tile made an immediate impact upon architects of that period. D&M tile designs may be viewed today at the unique Mission Inn in Riverside, California, and in a number of structures in San Diego's Balboa Park. "It was that inviting entry with its authentic tile work and the view straight through several rooms out to the sea that were so utterly appealing and reassuring, and I knew that I had to make the cottage my own," says Diane.

Entry through **stained-glass pocket doors** **reveal a** dining area contrasting strong **Monterey furniture** against **cream-washed walls**.

Aside from the children's rooms that are filled with color and whimsy, the home's rooms are uncluttered. Diane is fond of early California architecture, early California art and interior accompaniments. She is also a passionate advocate of the preservation of early California spaces and structures, and provides great energy and support to a number of organizations, including the Los Angeles Conservancy.

Entry through stained-glass pocket doors reveal a dining area contrasting strong Monterey furniture against cream-washed walls. Staircases with D&M tile abound throughout the cottage.

In staying with the true classic cottage fashion, Diane will tell you that it's as important that her dog feel as comfortable in her home as does her family. So it is with Red, the protector of the domain. Red is a rescue dog and a Texas native. (Besides having an unbounded passion for historic preservation, there is no greater advocate of animal rescue and adoption than Diane. She is a spokesperson for the Helen Woodward Animal Center, one of America's great animal-related educational and therapeutic facilities.)

Diane has found in Shaw's Cove an unmatched blend of authenticity and comfort—a true Pacific Coast vintage cottage. ◆

LEFT: Lively and playful colors make this children's room both inviting and warm.
ABOVE: An original Hardy Boys adventure *Hunting for Hidden Gold*, first published the year the cottage was built, sits with early-twentieth-century toy trucks, a primitive oil painting and a hooked rug in the children's room.

Conroy Cottage

EVERY VISITOR IS CHEERFULLY greeted at the front gate to this airy and updated 1930 cottage by boxers Bert and Ernie. "We try to walk them about five miles each day," says owner Deb Conroy. "After those walks, all their energy is converted into graceful prances across the property." And what a fun property it is. Lined with a period picket fence and anchored by an arbor topped with yellow roses, this 1,050-square-foot home sits back from a quiet lane, allowing a well-proportioned yard to frame the cottage. Visitors follow a flagstone path up to the wrap-around porch, upgraded in 2000, which provides a perfect resting spot for Deb and her husband, Dan, as well as their pups. During the winter, they make convenient use of a stand-up heat lamp in order to maintain the outdoor-indoor use of their home year-round.

Entry is made directly from the porch into the spacious living room where powerful dark Brazilian hardwood floors contrast with the cream-washed walls. The focus is on a spectacular stone fireplace that, according to Dan, gets constant play between October and April. "We keep the wood burning at a moderate and constant level—just enough to remove the dampness of fog rolling in from the sea and the chill that works its way up from nearby canyons." Deb

Clean and colorful lines add the perfect touch to the living room. A vintage early-twentieth-century still life floral sits atop an English pine cabinet.

has added excitement to the room with a 1930s-like olive-colored club couch positioned opposite a coral-colored club chair. The original Conroy clan hailed from Kilkenny, Ireland, and to ensure the incorporation of those family lines into this American cottage, an Irish pine cabinet anchors a nearby wall. Leaning above it is a nineteenth-century floral oil painting that Deb found on one of her antique hunts.

"We've made sure in the design, arrangements and upgrade of various rooms that they remain true to the period and more importantly that each of them is fully functional and comfortable. We use and enjoy every room!" Deb notes.

Around the corner from the living room, through a period arched hallway entrance, guests are treated to an updated classic cottage kitchen and dining area. Granite countertops,

OPPOSITE: A newly built garden expands the livable space of the cottage. LEFT: The expansive porch is a modern addition to the 1930 cottage and has provided the house with a new dimension. TOP: Bert and Ernie are eager to greet all guests. ABOVE: A periwinkle door contrasts beautifully against old brick.

Visitors follow a flagstone path up to the wraparound porch, which provides a perfect resting spot for Deb and her husband, Dan, as well as their pups.

stainless appliances and a professional-grade range and oven are not there just for show. Deb and Dan, both avid chefs, spend a great deal of time in the kitchen cooking for family and friends and simply coming up with new and exciting recipes on quiet weekend afternoons. The built-in cabinets are all custom, and the unusual sink is actually a vintage farmhouse sink that Deb found in England. "The inclusion of the vintage sink was intended to counterbalance the sleakness of the stainless appliances and granite countertops, and to ensure a sense of warmth and humility to the kitchen." When the dining area, perfect for six guests, is the scene of a Conroy dinner party, the french doors just off the kitchen are opened, allowing the party to flow into a backyard redwood deck and garden. "The cottage is all about friends," says Dan. "We love to entertain and particularly enjoy when guests make full use of the property."

The master bedroom and bath are sanctuaries of a sort. With walls washed in a Hawthorne yellow, the room is filled with sunlight from a unique sixteen-pane window and nearby french doors leading into the

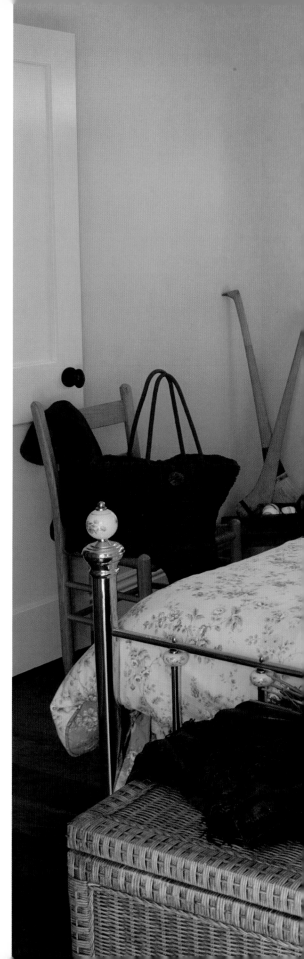

ABOVE: A late-nineteenth-century still life acts as a backdrop for Deb's vintage pottery. RIGHT: The brass bed adds a late-nineteenth-century feel to the bright yet warm master bedroom. OVERLEAF, LEFT: The table is set with vintage dog china, and the arched doorway provides a peek at the stone living room fireplace. OVERLEAF, RIGHT: The cottage is the venue for scrumptious dinner parties, and the kitchen is a favorite gathering spot for guests seeking an early taste of the dinner to come.

backyard. "The brass bed, that we swore early on we'd replace, has been with us for fifteen years and looks as though it's a keeper," says Deb. "We're giving thought to installing a vintage Franklin stove in the room, and if that happens I know I'll never leave!"

Around the corner is a guest bedroom with walls washed in a cranberry hue. Adjacent to the guest room is a guest bathroom that holds special charm. A vintage claw-foot tub and pedestal sink are positioned over a clean white hexagonal tile floor typical of the 1930s; all are surrounded by simple yet elegant tongue-and-groove walls. "After a hard day at work and a five-mile walk with Bert and Ernie, there's nothing better than settling into that tub with the sounds of Josh Groban in the background," exclaims Deb.

An old Irish proverb reminds us that "The smaller the cabin, the wider the door." So it is with Conroy Cottage—a home built from friendship, love and an abiding sense of pride. ◆

OPPOSITE: A bold red guest room is a perfect contrast to the other colors throughout the cottage. ABOVE: After a long day at work, this vintage claw-foot tub is Deb's favorite destination. The patterned octagonal floor tile has been recently added to bring back the feel of the period.

Pelican Roost

STARTING IN 1927 as a simple one-bedroom home with an unattached back unit, this seaside cottage has, during the course of some very careful upgrades, been unified and transformed into a lovely Craftsman bungalow. Tasteful earth tones and trim highlight the cottage's exterior. True to the American Craftsman tradition, the house is anchored by a mixed material chimney composed of both brick and river rock. Embedded within the brick are handcrafted stone tiles depicting chestnuts and maple leaves reminiscent of tiles fired by Pasadena artisan Ernest Batchelder in the 1920s.

A young and very friendly German shepherd, whom we addressed as Shep, greeted us the day we visited Pelican Roost. Entry to the property is made through an Arts and Crafts fence to a well-proportioned yard. "We've landscaped with self-sufficiency in mind. Rather than attend to the staging of annuals, we've elected to go with perennials that are indigenous to our region, and we think it works well with the Craftsman design," says the owner. The extended front porch is in keeping with the American Craftsman style. Positioned in front of the doorway on the porch is a pair of comfortable Adirondack chairs with cushions designed in a fabric pattern consistent

The contrasting colors and tones of the cottage work perfectly with the early-twentieth-century architecture and includes porch features indicative of the period. The owner's dog, affectionately called Shep, waits for another round of "catch."

with the period. "We live in a part of town that is comprised primarily of small turn-of-the-century cottages and bungalows, and all of us take great pride in our neighborhood. We enjoy sitting on the porch and greeting friends from time to time while enjoying a cup of coffee." It was also clear that Shep enjoys the porch as much as his owners.

The living room walls, partly earth-toned board and batten and partly white tongue and groove, play beautifully against the original oak floors. Anchoring the living room is a brick fireplace with a strongly colored wooden mantel upon which is angled a vintage mirror fronted by the owner's art and collectibles. Embedded within the fireplace's

OPPOSITE: The original kitchen has been upgraded and is complete with its original tin ceiling. LEFT: A colorful table is set with vintage pottery and garden-picked zinnias in the dining area and looks out into an adjoining courtyard. A warm-toned dog painting by the owner overlooks the table. TOP: Vintage collectibles front a leaded-glass window in the kitchen. ABOVE: Close-up of a vintage California tile lined along the fireplace mantel.

We've built a simple life in a historic, authentic and sustainable community, and we consider ourselves fortunate to be part of it.

fascia is a series of colorful 1930s tiles, an additional American Craftsman touch. The series augments a collection of original art tiles that are displayed in one of the bookcases. The living room is punctuated by two spectacular Paul Frankl art deco six-band rattan chairs and matching table, all of which were first introduced by the furniture designer in the late 1920s.

An avid reader, the owner has a prized collection of first editions by L. Frank Baum tucked within a living room bookcase. Baum, originally from upstate New York and the son of a wealthy businessman, dabbled in theater, printing, newspaper reporting and retail before inking *The Wonderful World of Oz* in 1900. He went on (with illustrator W. W. Denslow) to write thirteen additional children's books about life in the Land of Oz, and his legacy as a beloved author was thereafter and forever sealed.

An avid reader, the owner has a prized collection of first editions by L. Frank Baum tucked within a living room bookcase.

Connected to the front cottage by a breezeway, the back cottage houses an artist's studio where the owner spends much of her time when not otherwise focusing on commitments to the town in which she lives. "We've built a simple life in a historic, authentic and sustainable community, and we consider ourselves fortunate to be part of it," says the owner. Pelican Roost was a joy to visit, and it stands as a fine example of a classic American bungalow that will remain a part of the community legacy for years to come. ◆

Painters Cottage and Fisherman's Perch

THESE TWO CLASSIC seaside cottages are part of the Crystal Cove State Park Historic District, which includes forty-six rustic cottages that are listed on the National Register of Historic Places. Built between 1920 and 1940, these cottages represent a bygone era of simpler times along the California Coast and are recognized as being the last intact examples of early vernacular architecture. The history of all the cottages is beautifully and authoritatively captured in *Crystal Cove Cottages: Islands in Time on the California Coast*, written by Karen E. Steen, Laura Davick and Meriam Braselle.

The recently restored cottages are in part a result of the passion and vision of Laura Davick, a third-generation "coveite." As president and founder of the nonprofit Crystal Cove Alliance, she continues her mission to raise funds and to identify sources of private funding for the restoration of the remaining twenty-four cottages. On April 5, 2006, Crystal Cove Alliance was awarded a concession contract by California State Parks to manage the overnight rentals and food service. In

The sitting porch doubles as a studio and faces the sea. Its location provides comfort as well as inspiration.

Built between 1920 and 1940, these cottages represent a bygone era of simpler times along the California Coast and are recognized as being the last intact examples of early vernacular architecture.

June 2006, fourteen of the twenty-two restored cottages were opened to the public as overnight rentals. One of the restored cottages was converted to a restaurant, aptly named the Beachcomber at Crystal Cove. The nearby Shake Shack, located on Pacific Coast Highway, continues to make sandwiches and date shakes, something that they have grown famous for decades. For additional information about the cottages, visit www.crystalcovealliance.org.

The two cottages featured in this section were photographed prior to the completion of the transformation. I wish to thank Laura Davick and Ken Kramer, Crystal Cove State Park superintendent, for providing a peek inside these wonderful structures before they were converted to public use.

PAINTERS COTTAGE

A board-and-batten structure, the primary living area overlooks a wide beach and the Pacific Ocean. The west-facing sleeping porch has served as both a place of rest as well as an artist's studio. For this reason, it is now affectionately referred to as the Painters Cottage. The exterior of the cottage is a clean whitewash paint accented with forest green trim, a traditional cottage favorite.

The bentwood rocker, also in a forest green, is a perfect match for the outside portion of the cottage. Just to the south, the porch has been enclosed with a large set of windows that open to the outside porch and a triple set of nine-pane windows that look toward the sea. The enclosed porch-studio is anchored with oak hardwood flooring. Resting on a nearby vintage easel is a 1930s plein air

OPPOSITE: A 1920s Roseville vase and arrangement of French tulips sits adjacent a seascape most likely painted by a former owner. ABOVE: A bentwood chair and side table with camp blanket sit adjacent an early-twentieth-century cabinet against one wall of the living room. Upon the cabinet are shells from family trips and the local shore.

THIS PAGE: Just inside the porch is the pine-walled and hard-wood-floor living room original to the cottage. An unusually colored lifesaver hangs just above the colorful 1930s dining table and chairs. OPPOSITE: This name plate displays the original name of the cabin.

painting of the California Coast. The main living room, just a step inside the enclosed porch, is walled in a wide-planked vintage pine. On the north side of the room, nearest the kitchen, is a classic round wood table surrounded by mission-style chairs that were long ago painted orange but now are faded. Against a nearby wall hangs an old canvas life preserver painted in classic green. Across the room, a large vintage cabinet washed in a faded sea-foam green is covered with seashells from California.

Early California oil paintings are displayed on each side of the cabinet. "Plein air paintings were an important part of the history of Crystal Cove," says Laura Davick. "At the end of each summer, we are continuing this tradition with our 'Coastal Splendor' Plein Air Invitational, a plein air competition that draws award-winning artists both locally and from around the country to participate in our annual Tropical Gala fund-raising event." The event is judged by Jean Stern, executive director of the Irvine Museum.

Artist prize money is generously donated by Joan Irvine Smith Fine Arts. Revenue raised from the sale of these magnificent plein air paintings continues to support their mission of education and restoration.

The east wall of the living room is accented by a vintage 1930s sunflower quilt and a classic rattan floor lamp from Hawaii.

Across a doorway, on the other end of the east wall, is an old wicker desk lighted by a late 1920s coconut lamp, also from Hawaii. Just above the desk and to the right of the lamp is a prized keepsake, a 1940s painting of a local fishing boat exhibiting the quick strokes and intense colors of early California artist Anders Gustave Aldrin. ◆

An old wicker desk is lighted by a late 1920s coconut lamp from Hawaii. Just above the desk is a prized keepsake, a 1940s painting of a local fishing boat exhibiting the quick strokes and intense colors of early California artist Anders Gustave Aldrin.

FISHERMAN'S PERCH

Entry to the main living area is made, as in the case of Painters Cottage, by way of a narrow staircase leading up the hill to the cottage. The enclosed porch leads into a room with vaulted wood-beam ceilings and vintage plank pine walls. The south wall is anchored by a small rustic fireplace. Just above the fireplace are vintage lithographs of game fish. On the stove affixed to the fireplace is a 1930s partially completed sailboat hull. Inside the hull is an envelope dated November 25, 1937, upon which is sketched a detailed design of the full boat. The envelope also contains paper templates to aid in its construction. What a keepsake! Tucked into a nearby corner are two classic 1920s hand-crafted speedboats. Inside the lower boat is an article from the May 1927 edition of *Popular Science Monthly* entitled "A Boy Can Build This Boat" by Frederick P. Berrian. It begins:

ABOVE: Sitting atop the fireplace are early fishing prints and a hand-carved, partially completed pond boat hull dating to 1937. RIGHT: The pine-walled and vaulted-ceiling living room emphasizes seaside comfort with an early-twentieth-century wicker couch that sits below a bold seascape. Early prints sit above the fireplace. In the corner are two motorized pond boats, both from the late 1920s.

"Just mention motor boats to a boy and see the broad smile that lights his face. That's true, too, of many men, for there is something exceedingly fascinating about a toy motor boat that will run speedily under its own power." The article goes on with instructions for the crafting of a sleuth, including scale drawings. It is a great example of the fact that in the heyday of this classic cottage, the most valued items were hand made, not store bought.

Anchoring the east wall is a colorful 1930s oil painting of the nearby coast by an unknown artist. Located in the living area on vintage tables is a pair of 1940s cypress knees lamps that lend a warm hue to the room. Laura notes, "Long before I was born, stories abounded of the casual lifestyle at the cove. It doesn't take much to imagine how idyllic it must have been with a two-lane highway that was barely traveled and an overwhelming sense of quiet that was broken only by the sound of gulls and the sea!"

As we left both cottages, I couldn't help but think of some lyrics from the great American sea chantey *Sail Away Ladies*:

> *Ever I get my new house done,*
> *Give my old one to my son,*
> *Ever I finish this porch and stairs,*
> *Lie around in my rockin' chair.* ◆

OPPOSITE: From the coat rack hangs a quilt and two Pendleton jackets. Above are old family trophies and a primitive seascape that was likely constructed over a long summer by the original owner and which is framed with tiny seashells and pinecones. LEFT: A vintage owl weathervane looks seaward and stands next to a vintage table readied with fresh fruit for hungry swimmers. TOP: The beach chaise is the perfect spot for an early afternoon nap on the covered porch. ABOVE: A game board is always at the ready at Fisherman's Perch.